EDGE BOOKS

A FIELD GUIDE TO
Elves, Dwarves,
AND OTHER Magical Folk

BY A. J. SAUTTER

CAPSTONE PRESS
a capstone imprint

Edge Books are published by Capstone Press,
1710 Roe Crest Drive, North Mankato, Minnesota 56003
www.capstonepub.com

Library of Congress Cataloging-in-Publication Data
Sautter, Aaron.
A field guide to elves, dwarves, and other magical folk / by A.J. Sautter.
pages cm.—(Edge books. Fantasy field guides)
Includes bibliographical references and index.
Summary: "Describes the features and characteristics of magical fantasy creatures in
a quick-reference format"—Provided by publisher.
ISBN 978-1-4914-0692-2 (library binding)
ISBN 978-1-4914-0696-0 (paperback)
ISBN 978-1-4914-0700-4 (eBook PDF)
1. Fairies—Juvenile literature. 2. Elves—Juvenile literature. 3. Dwarves—Juvenile
literature. 4. Gnomes—Juvenile literature. I. Title.
GR549.S28 2015
398.21—dc23   2014010192

Editorial Credits
Sarah Bennett, designer; Kazuko Collins, layout artist;
Kelly Garvin, media researcher; Katy LaVigne, production specialist

Photo Credits
Alamy Images/Paz Spinelli, 27; Capstone Press: Colin Ashcroft, 1, 8, 14, Jason
Juta, 17, 19, Martin Bustamante, cover, 11, 13, 20, 23, Mike Nash, 7; Dreamstime/
ateliersommerland, 25; Shutterstock: dalmingo, 28, Elena Schweitzer, 4-5

Artistic Credits
Shutterstock: argus, foxie, homydesign, Kompaniets Taras, Lora liu, Oleg Golovnev,
Picsfire, Rashevska Nataliia, xpixel

Printed in the United States of America in Stevens Point, Wisconsin.
052014   008092WZF14

Table of Contents

A World of
Magical People

Have you ever walked in the woods and noticed something moving at the corner of your eye? Maybe it was a squirrel running behind a tree or a colorful dragonfly flittering among the leaves. Or could it have been something more mysterious and magical? Maybe what you saw was a fairy, a gnome, or an elf hiding in the shadows. After all, many **myths** talk about magical folk living in a world hidden beyond our own.

Could these stories be describing actual creatures? The truth is that elves, centaurs, merfolk, and other magical beings live only in our imaginations. Stories about them have been told for hundreds of years. Long ago people thought creatures like brownies or fairies were responsible for unexplainable events. Today we know these magical creatures don't exist. But they're more popular than ever. They show up in books, movies, TV shows, and more. Why do we keep telling stories about them? Maybe because we wish they were real. These fantastic creatures help us feel that there's still some mystery in the real world.

Let's imagine that elves, fairies, and other magical folk are real and alive in the world today. If you wanted to find them, would you know where to look? What do they eat? How should you act if you meet one? Get ready for an amazing adventure as you learn about these magical people and how they might live if they were real.

myth ⋯ a story told by people in ancient times

Centaurs

Size:
about 7 to 7.5 feet
(2.1 to 2.3 meter) tall

Habitat:
forests, plains, and foothills
near mountains

Diet:
meat, grains, fruits,
vegetables, bread, cheese

Life Cycle: Female centaurs give birth once every three to four years. Most female centaurs have six to eight children during their lifetimes. Young centaurs grow quickly and reach adulthood by the age of 5. Centaurs don't live in regular families. They instead live as part of a herd. Each centaur works to care for and protect the herd. Most centaurs live to be about 75 years old.

Physical Features: Centaurs are part human and part horse. Their human upper bodies are strong and muscular. Almost all centaurs have shoulder-length hair. Some males also grow bushy beards. Centaurs' powerful, horselike lower bodies are usually covered in dark brown or black hair.

Behavior: Centaurs tend to be **arrogant**. They often think they are better than others. For this reason, centaurs normally keep to themselves and rarely make friends with outsiders. However, centaurs are extremely loyal to their few friends. They will gladly risk their lives to help friends in need. Most centaurs have excellent skills with bows, swords, and spears and are deadly during a fight.

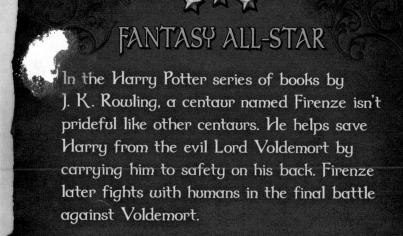

★ ★ ★
FANTASY ALL-STAR

In the Harry Potter series of books by J. K. Rowling, a centaur named Firenze isn't prideful like other centaurs. He helps save Harry from the evil Lord Voldemort by carrying him to safety on his back. Firenze later fights with humans in the final battle against Voldemort.

arrogant ··· exaggerating one's own self-worth or importance, often in an overbearing manner

Satyrs

Size
about 5 to 5.5 feet
(1.5 to 1.7 m) tall

Habitat:
thick forests and
hilly regions near
mountains

Diet:
fruits, vegetables,
bread, cheese, wine

Life Cycle: Female satyrs usually have two babies every three or four years. Satyr children grow about as fast as human children do. They are considered adults by age 15. Like centaurs, satyrs don't live in families like humans. Instead most live in small tribes that wander their territory together. It is unknown how long satyrs live, but it's thought they can live for several hundred years.

Physical Features: Satyrs have the legs and feet of goats with upper bodies similar to those of humans. Satyr heads and faces are a combination of human and goatlike features. They have long narrow noses and large curved horns. Most satyrs also have long whiskers growing from their chins. Satyrs' bodies are usually completely covered in coarse brown or gray hair.

Behavior: Satyrs are known for enjoying good parties. They like nothing better than gathering together and having lots of fun. Satyrs love beautiful things found in nature. They spend much of their time exploring forests to find flowers or beautiful views they haven't seen before. Satyrs are also skilled musicians. Many satyrs learn to play **panpipes** at a young age. They often use their pipes to cast magic musical spells. These spells are usually used for entertaining friends at parties. But if they feel threatened, satyrs may use their musical spells to confuse enemies or put them to sleep.

panpipe ⋯ a musical instrument made of several hollow pipes of various lengths

Fairies

Size:
in magical form fairies
are the size of insects;
in their true form, fairies
are about 4.5 to 5 feet
(1.4 to 1.5 m) tall

Habitat:
woodland areas
filled with streams
and meadows

Diet:
berries, fruits,
vegetables, sweet
flowers

Life Cycle: Fairies always appear to be female. Nobody
has ever seen a male fairy. It's thought that fairy children are
born from moonflower blossoms under the light of a full moon
on **Midsummer's Eve**. Fairy children reach adulthood by age 7.
After this point they seem to stop aging. Fairies always appear
youthful, even if they are thousands of years old.

Physical Features: In magical form fairies appear as
butterflies, moths, dragonflies, and other colorful flying
insects. But in their true form, fairies appear as beautiful young
women with long wavy hair. Fairies are best known for the
large **gossamer** wings attached to their backs. The wings are
lightweight, yet are very strong.

Behavior: Fairies use their magical form to hide their true
appearance. They reveal their true form only to those they
trust. But in spite of their shy nature, fairies are curious and
like to explore the world around them. When they meet
people, they are friendly, talkative, and outgoing. However,
fairies are easily angered by those who harm the natural world.
They'll use their magic to scare off anyone they feel
is a threat to nature.

Midsummer's Eve ⇥ a holiday celebrating
the longest day of the year
gossamer ⇥ thin, light, and delicate

Brownies

Size:
about 8 to 12 inches (20 to 30 centimeters) tall

Habitat:
crawlspaces, attics, and other small spaces in barns and farmhouses

Diet:
bread, milk, cheese, porridge with honey

Life Cycle: Brownie mothers have one baby about every four to five years. Young brownies grow quickly and are considered adults by age 10. However, adult brownies age slowly. The oldest known brownie lived to be more than 600 years old.

Physical Features: Brownies are short **humanoid** creatures that appear somewhat ratlike. They have beady black eyes, pointed ears and noses, whiskers, and strong front teeth. Their hands and feet are often covered with tough **calluses** from the work they do around the house. Brownies usually wear shabby clothes made from scraps of cloth or old doll clothes that they find.

Behavior: Also known as house elves, brownies don't like to be seen by humans. However, they are very friendly. They often do household chores during the night such as mending clothes, cleaning dishes, and mopping floors. They never expect payment for their work. But they do enjoy small gifts of food, milk, or shiny trinkets. However, brownies are easily offended if someone criticizes their work. Once insulted, they may undo the work they've done or make large messes to get back at those who offended them.

FANTASY ALL-STAR

A brownie named Thimbletack plays a large role in The Spiderwick Chronicles series by Tony DiTerlizzi and Holly Black. When an ogre tries to take over the world, Thimbletack helps his human friends defeat the monster.

humanoid -·- shaped somewhat like a human

callus -·- a thickened and hardened part of the skin

Gnomes

Size:
about 18 to 24 inches
(46 to 61 cm) tall

Habitat:
small caves and
hollow trees in hilly
wooded areas

Diet:
fruit, mushrooms,
nuts, beans,
vegetables, honey

Life Cycle: Gnomes have families much like humans do. Most families include a father, mother, and up to five children. Gnome women have one baby about every five years. Gnome children grow slowly and are not considered adults until about age 45. Adult gnomes can live up to 500 years. They appear to age normally, but they remain strong and active throughout their lives.

Physical Features: Although shorter than dwarves, gnomes are often mistaken for them. Gnomes usually have stocky bodies. Their strong hands often show signs of doing hard work in their underground mines and workshops. Adult males usually grow long white or gray beards. A few gnomes occasionally wear pointed red or green hats. But they usually prefer not to wear anything on their heads.

Behavior: Gnomes are quiet, shy, and peaceful. They like to keep to themselves and have little contact with people. Gnomes are **stealthy** and can avoid being seen by others. However, they are on friendly terms with elves, fairies, and other people who respect nature. Most gnomes spend their days gathering food or mining for gemstones underground. They are also skilled craftsmen. Gnomes are known for creating some of the finest gems and jewelry available.

Fact According to some myths, gnomes were small earth spirits that guarded treasures in underground caves or mines. It was thought that gnomes could move through solid earth as easily as birds move through the air.

stealthy ⋯ able to move secretly and quietly

Halflings

Size:
about 3 to 3.5 feet (0.9 to 1 m) tall

Habitat:
dry underground holes featuring the comforts of home; some halflings build small homes near lakes or rivers

Diet:
meat, cheese, mushrooms, vegetables, fruit, bread, honey

Life Cycle:
Halflings live in families just like humans do. However, halfling families are usually very large. Couples commonly have 15 or more children. Halfling children grow as fast as human children, but they are not considered adults until about age 30. Most halflings live between 90 and 100 years. A few have lived up to 130 years.

Physical Features:
Halflings are about half the size of humans. Almost all halflings have curly brown hair. Halfling men don't grow beards, but a few may have bushy sideburns framing their round faces. All halflings have large, tough feet covered in furry brown hair. They never wear shoes or boots.

Behavior:
Halflings are peaceful people who like to keep to themselves. They prefer a quiet life, good food, and the comforts of home. They often eat five or six meals a day. But in spite of their soft and easygoing lifestyle, halflings are tough. They can overcome many hardships and difficulties when necessary. Halflings can also be very stealthy. They seem to have a magical ability to move in total silence to avoid being seen by others.

★ ★ ★ FANTASY ALL-STAR

In *The Hobbit* and *The Lord of the Rings* by J.R.R. Tolkien, halflings are known as hobbits. Bilbo and Frodo Baggins are two hobbits who each go on difficult adventures. In spite of their small size, they are both very brave and help defeat terrible forces of evil.

16

Dwarves

Size:
4 to 4.5 feet
(1.2 to 1.4 m) tall

Habitat:
amazing cities built inside
huge mountain caves

Diet:
meat, potatoes, grains,
fruits, bread, cheese, wine

Life Cycle: Outsiders rarely see dwarf women and children. For this reason, some people mistakenly believe that dwarves grow right out of the ground. But dwarves have families like other people do. Dwarf children are born only about every 25 years. They grow slowly and don't reach adulthood until about age 50. Dwarves have long lifespans and often reach at least 250 years of age. Some dwarves may even live up to 350 years.

Physical Features: Dwarves are short, but they make up for it with their thickly muscled bodies. They are much stronger than humans and can carry heavy loads over long distances. As dwarves age their skin becomes thicker and tougher, resulting in lumpy ears and noses. Dwarf men take great pride in their long beards. They often weave and braid their beards into fantastic designs that reflect their personalities.

Behavior: Dwarves spend much of their time mining for gold, silver, gems, and other treasures. They are also expert craftsmen. Few people can match the quality of their weapons, armor, and jewelry. A few dwarves are also skilled at creating magical weapons and armor that are highly valued by most warriors. Dwarves are proud and noble people. Because of past conflicts, most dwarves don't like or trust elves. Dwarves are usually friendly toward humans, halflings, and gnomes. However, dwarves are fiercely private about their personal lives. If asked too many questions about their families, dwarves may become offended. They will suddenly end the conversation and simply walk away.

Elves

Size:
6 to 6.5 feet
(1.8 to 2 m) tall

Habitat:
forests and peaceful
mountain valleys

Diet:
fruits, vegetables, grains,
bread, honey, wine

Life Cycle: Most elves have only one or two children during their entire lifetime. Elf children's minds develop very quickly. They can speak, read, dance, and recite poetry by age 2. However, elf children physically grow very slowly. They are not considered adults until about age 100. Elves do not get sick or grow old. They can be killed in battle, but they are otherwise **immortal**.

Physical Features: Elves have tall, slender bodies that make them seem weak and delicate. However, they are actually quite strong and athletic. Elves are known for their flawless skin and attractive appearance. They have long, straight hair that is normally blonde. Only a few are known to have dark brown or red hair. Elves are best known for their pointed ears, bright eyes, and smiling faces.

Behavior: Elves are generally peaceful people with great respect for nature. In fact, only fairies form a closer bond with animals and trees than elves do. Elves also have a great love of the arts. They spend much of their free time creating poetry, music, and fine crafts. But when the need arises, elves can also be fearsome warriors. Their battle skills and magical weapons and armor are unmatched by anyone. Elves are very loyal to their friends. They'll always come to the aid of their friends, no matter how dangerous the situation is.

immortal ⋯ able to live forever

Dark Elves

Size:
5.5 to 6 feet
(1.7 to 1.8 m) tall

Habitat:
large cities deep
under the earth

Diet:
lizards, lizard eggs, rats,
fish, insects, mushrooms

Life Cycle: Dark elves have children every four to five years. Dark elf children are intelligent. But because of the violent nature of dark elf **society**, many children don't live to adulthood. Like elves that live above ground, dark elves do not age or die of natural causes. But they often die fighting in battles or through other violent methods.

Physical Features: Like their cousins above ground, dark elves have slender bodies, pointed ears, and are usually very good looking. However, dark elves are known for their very dark skin and straight white hair. Their eyes are commonly red or yellow. But in rare cases a dark elf may have dark blue or purple eyes.

Behavior: Dark elves live in a dangerous and violent world. Dark elf society seems to be in a constant state of war. Strong families often battle one another for power and control over their underground cities. From the moment they begin to walk, dark elf children are taught the art of fighting and war. Whether using swords or powerful magic spells, most dark elves enjoy attacking and killing their enemies. Dark elves often **raid** rival cities and surface villages to steal food, supplies, and people to work as slaves.

★ ★ ★ FANTASY ALL-STAR

Drizzt Do'Urden is a popular dark elf featured in many books by author R.A. Salvatore. Drizzt rejects his people's evil ways and chooses to live with honor and respect toward others. He is a highly skilled warrior who uses his fighting skills to help protect his friends.

society ⇢ a group that shares the same laws and customs

raid ⇢ to make a sudden, surprise attack on a place

Merfolk

Size:
about 7 feet
(2.1 m) long

Habitat:
shallow seas near
tropical coasts; some
deep inland lakes

Diet:
fish, clams, oysters,
crabs, shrimp, some
types of seaweed

Life Cycle: Merfolk usually have one child every two years. Young merfolk grow quickly. They can care for themselves by age 8 and are considered adults by age 10. Merfolk families are very close. Most young adults don't leave home until they're 25 to 30 years old. Most merfolk live about 200 years.

Physical Features: From the waist up, merfolk appear similar to humans. They have fair skin and athletic upper bodies. Instead of ears, merfolk have **gills** that allow them to breathe underwater. Merfolk usually have waist-length hair that is blonde, light brown, or red. Their lower bodies are like that of a large fish with deep blue or green scales. Their tails end in a large fin or flipper used to quickly swim through the water.

Behavior: Merfolk don't like intruders and fiercely protect their territories. If sailors happen to spot merfolk, these beings may at first seem friendly and playful. They'll smile and motion the sailors to follow them. But merfolk usually use this scheme to lead ships away from their hidden cities. Once at a safe distance, the merfolk simply disappear and swim away under the water.

It's thought that some merfolk can transform their fishy tails into normal human legs. This ability allows them to briefly walk on land for up to 12 hours. But merfolk can't travel too far from the water. If on land for too long, they can't change back to their natural form. For this reason, most merfolk don't walk on land. They can't bear the idea of being separated from their families forever.

gill — a body part on a fish used to breathe underwater

24

Treefolk

Size:
30 to 40 feet
(9 to 12 m) tall

Habitat:
thick forests with
many trees

Diet:
unknown, but
probably water
rich in nutrients

Life Cycle: All known treefolk are adult males. It's unknown how these creatures reproduce. Some people think they grow from nuts or acorns until they are old enough to guard their forest homes. Treefolk live for thousands of years and are the oldest of all known magical creatures. The oldest known treeman is at least 10,000 years old.

Physical Features: Treefolk look very much like trees. They have thick trunklike legs, and their arms and hands look like tree branches. Their feet look like tree roots spread out on the ground, and their skin is similar to thick, rough bark. Most treefolk have wise-looking green or yellow-brown eyes. Treefolk usually have large, crooked noses, and some have beards made of vines or moss.

Behavior: Treefolk are the guardians of the forest. They spend their days protecting trees from being cut down. Some treefolk also enjoy writing poems and telling long stories. Because of their long lives, treefolk are extremely slow in almost everything they do. They speak very slowly, and they can take an entire day to make even minor decisions. However, if they are stirred to anger, treefolk can be fearsome. They are incredibly strong and can easily tear down a large stone **fortress** in less than a day.

fortress -- a place that is built to be strong and well defended against attacks

★ ★ ★
FANTASY ALL-STAR

In *The Lord of the Rings*, treefolk are called ents. The chief and oldest ent is named Treebeard. He leads a group of ents to fight an orc army and stop the plans of the evil wizard Saruman.

Legends Around the World

𝔉 Fairies

Ancient myths and stories of fairylike creatures can be found all over Europe. They are most commonly found in Great Britain. Famous stories featuring fairies include "Sir Orfeo," "Tam Lin," and the play *A Midsummer Night's Dream*.

𝔈, 𝔇 Elves and Dwarves

Myths and legends about elves and dwarves began mainly in Norse mythology from Scandinavia. They are found in collections of ancient stories called the *Poetic Edda* and the *Prose Edda*. Elves and dwarves also appear in short stories from *Grimm's Fairy Tales*, which was first published in Germany in 1812.

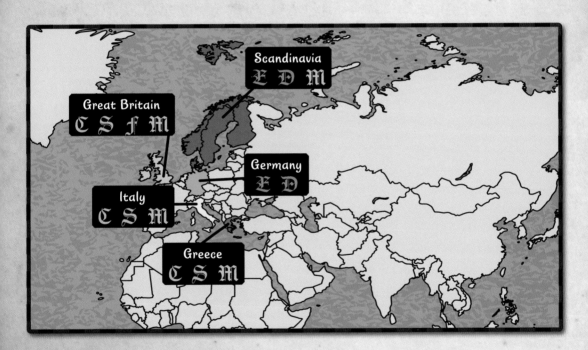

ℭ, 𝔖 Centaurs and Satyrs

Centaurs and satyrs have appeared in fantastic tales for thousands of years. These stories come mainly from Greek and Roman myths. In the late 1500s, William Shakespeare wrote about them in plays such as *A Midsummer Night's Dream*. They also remain popular in today's fantasy stories such as the Harry Potter and Percy Jackson series of books.

𝔐 Merfolk

Stories featuring merfolk can be found from England to China. Merfolk are seen in many myths and legends of ancient Greece and Rome. They are often described as being dangerous in tales from Great Britain. Written in Denmark in 1837, *The Little Mermaid* is probably the most famous story featuring merfolk.

Test Your Knowledge

Do you feel you know all there is to know about elves, fairies, and other magical people? Test your knowledge with this short quiz. Do you have what it takes to become an expert on magical fantasy creatures?

1 **You wake up to find your kitchen is completely clean, but the dishes are not put away. You suspect that brownies are responsible. Should you:**

A. leave a gift of clothing?

B. leave a gift of food or milk?

C. leave a note to explain how to put away the dishes?

2 **Halflings are naturally:**

A. loud and clumsy.

B. curious and adventurous.

C. quiet and stealthy.

3 **Dwarves are not normally friendly with:**

A. elves.

B. humans.

C. satyrs.

4 **Which folk make the best quality weapons and armor?**

A. dwarves

B. gnomes

C. elves

5 **Merfolk can walk on land up to:**

A. 12 days.

B. 12 hours.

C. 12 weeks.

6 **Satyrs love to:**

A. eat, drink, and play music at parties.

B. spend quiet evenings at home.

C. craft magical weapons and armor.

Glossary

arrogant (AIR-uh-guhnt) ⸱⸱- exaggerating one's own self-worth or importance, often in an overbearing manner

callus (KAL-uhs) ⸱⸱- a thickened and hardened part of the skin

fortress (FOR-tress) ⸱⸱- a place that is built to be strong and well defended against attacks

gill (GIL) ⸱⸱- a body part on a fish used to breathe underwater

gossamer (GOSS-uh-mur) ⸱⸱- thin, light, and delicate

humanoid (HYOO-muh-noyd) ⸱⸱- shaped somewhat like a human

immortal (i-MOR-tuhl) ⸱⸱- able to live forever

Midsummer's Eve (MID-sum-uhrz EEV) ⸱⸱- a holiday celebrating the longest day of the year

myth (MITH) ⸱⸱- a story told by people in ancient times

panpipe (PAN-pipe) ⸱⸱- a musical instrument made of several hollow pipes of various lengths

raid (RAYD) ⸱⸱- to make a sudden, surprise attack on a place

society (suh-SYE-uh-tee) ⸱⸱- a group that shares the same laws and customs

stealthy (STEL-thee) ⸱⸱- able to move secretly and quietly

Read More

Berk, Ari. *The Secret History of Mermaids and Creatures of the Deep.* Somerville, Mass.: Candlewick Press, 2009.

Matthews, John. *How to See Fairies.* New York: Abrams, 2011.

Powel, Martin. *The Elves and the Shoemaker: A Grimm Graphic Novel.* Graphic Spin. Mankato, Minn.: Stone Arch Books, 2011.

Internet Sites

FactHound offers a safe, fun way to find Internet sites related to this book. All of the sites on FactHound have been researched by our staff.

Here's all you do:

Visit *www.facthound.com*

Type in this code: 9781491406922

 **Super-cool stuff!** Check out projects, games and lots more at **www.capstonekids.com**

Index